Unit 1

Practice until students can say the words individually without help.

1.  cockroach	2.  elephant	3.  giraffe	4.  lion
5.  cloud	6.  window	7.  sky	8.  colored pencils
9. 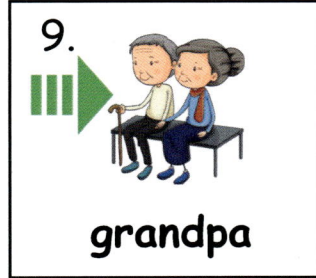 grandpa	10.  little sister	11.  little brother	12.  glue

Practice the questions together and then check in with students individually on their listening.

1. How are you?
2. What is your name?
3. How old are you?
4. Go get a pencil and eraser, please.
5. Look at me, please.
6. Sit properly, please.

Sign or Stamp

Reading Comprehension

Read, write and fill in the numbers. Then color.

1. This pig sits. 2. The cat jumps. 3. The dog runs. 4. The fish swims. They are having fun.

1. Practice as a class. 2. Practice individually. 3. Sign or stamp only when the student can read it on their own without help.

		Sight Word Review
ck	back	go
st	stop	he
ft	gift	they
sk	mask	you
nd	hand	she
ch	chop	watch
tch	catch	away
		one

Sign or Stamp

Students can work on this while you test them one on one on the previous page.

Write and find.

A	M	A	S	K	B	C	X	S	H	U	M
S	F	G	I	F	T	T	U	L	D	K	V
P	C	H	O	P	C	Y	Z	D	B	N	X
S	W	E	V	N	A	U	Y	Q	A	R	H
H	M	F	U	L	T	J	X	P	C	A	A
N	V	E	U	X	C	K	P	C	K	E	N
N	S	T	O	P	H	K	H	H	Q	N	D
L	T	H	E	Y	W	A	T	C	H	A	S

BACK   MASK   CATCH

STOP   HAND   THEY

GIFT   CHOP   WATCH

1. Practice as a class. 2. Practice individually. 3. Sign or stamp only when the student can read it on their own without help.

The disk went fast. The dog ran fast to catch the disk. Go, dog, go! The dog got it!

Sign or Stamp

Students can work on this while you test them one on one on the previous page.

Unit 2

Speaking Practice

Practice until students can say the words individually without help.

Are you _____?
Yes, I am.   No, I'm not.

1.  happy	2.  sad	3.  angry	4.  sick
5.  hungry	6.  thirsty	7.  tired	8.  excited

Listening Practice

Practice the questions together and then check in with students individually on their listening.

1. How are you?
2. What is your name?
3. What is your favorite color?
4. What is your favorite animal?
5. Who are the people in your family?
6. What do you like to eat?

Sign or Stamp

Reading Comprehension

Read, write and draw what is missing. Then color.

This is Jess. She is not sad. She sits in the sand. She sees a crab. The crab wants to grab an ant.

1. Practice as a class. 2. Practice individually. 3. Sign or stamp only when the student can read it on their own without help.

Sight Word Review

sh	shack
th	that
cl	clip
cr	crab
str	strip
qu	quit
ng	sing
le	little

are

want

find

what

when

see

goes

too

Sign or Stamp

Students can work on this while you test them one on one on the previous page.

Write and find.

SHACK　　　CRAB　　　SING

THAT　　　STRIP　　　LITTLE

CLIP　　　QUIT　　　WANT

1. Practice as a class. 2. Practice individually. 3. Sign or stamp only when the student can read it on their own without help.

The witch sings. The witch sings to the man. The man thinks that is bad, but he will not tell the witch!

Sign or Stamp

Students can work on this while you test them one on one on the previous page.

Unit 3

Speaking Practice
Practice until students can say the words individually without help.

Do you like _____?
Yes, I do. No, I don't.

1.  soup	2.  salad	3.  ice cream	4.  hot dogs
5.  hamburgers	6.  French fries	7.  fried chicken	8.  sandwiches

Listening Practice

Practice the questions together and then check in with students individually on their listening.

1. What do you like to eat?
2. Do you like sandwiches?
3. Do you like soup?
4. Are you hungry?
5. Are you thirsty?
6. Are you tired?

Sign or Stamp

Reading Comprehension
Read, write and color the rabbits the correct color.

The rabbits are in a band. One rabbit sings. It is a pink rabbit. One rabbit hits the drums. It is a black rabbit. Go, rabbits!

1. Practice as a class. 2. Practice individually. 3. Sign or stamp only when the student can read it on their own without help.

mat ➡ mate

mat
mate
fat
fate
rat
rate

Spelling Words:
fat
cake
take
two

Sight Words:
see
two

Sign or Stamp

Students can work on this while you test them one on one on the previous page.

Write and find.

MATE

BAKE

BLAME

FATE

TAKE

FLAME

CAKE

GAME

PLATE

1. Practice as a class. 2. Practice individually. 3. Sign or stamp only when the student can read it on their own without help.

He makes two big cakes. She sees the cakes and wants to take them. She jumps and…Splat!

Sign or Stamp

Students can work on this while you test them one on one on the previous page.

Unit 4

Speaking Practice

Practice until students can say the words individually without help.

What does your mom like to do? She likes to _____.

1.
talk

2.
cook

3.
exercise

4.
ride her bike

5.
watch movies

6.
go shopping

7.
work

8.
play with me

Listening Practice

Practice the questions together and then check in with students individually on their listening.

1. What does your mom like to do?
2. What does your dad like to do?
3. Does your dad like sandwiches?
4. Does your mom like hot dogs?
5. What do you like to do?

Sign or Stamp

Reading Comprehension
Read, write, draw and color.

Did this kid take some cake? Hmm. Yes. Did this dog take some cake? Hmm. Yes. I think the mom will be mad.

1. Practice as a class. 2. Practice individually. 3. Sign or stamp only when the student can read it on their own without help.

ai
ay

rain
train
main
day
say
play

Sight Words:
come
down

Spelling Words:
train
rain
day
play
come

Sign or Stamp

Students can work on this while you test them one on one on the previous page.

Write and find.

TRAIN	DAY	CLAIM
MAIN	SAY	COME
PLAIN	PLAY	DOWN

1. Practice as a class. 2. Practice individually. 3. Sign or stamp only when the student can read it on their own without help.

The man has a train. He wants to play with the train. He sits down on it. "Come on, train! Let's go!" But the train can't go.

Sign or Stamp

Students can work on this while you test them one on one on the previous page.

Review Assessments

A. Speaking

1. Practice as a class and in partners beforehand.
2. How many sentences can you make in a minute?

1. (question)
2. (answer)

3. (question)
4. (answer)

5. (question)
6. (answer)

7. (question)
8. (answer)

9. (question)
10. (answer)

11. (question)
12. (answer)

13. (question)
14. (answer)

15. (question)
16. (answer)

17. (question)
18. (answer)

19. (question)
20. (answer)

21. (question)
22. (answer)

23. (question)
24. (answer)

Review Assessments
B. Reading

How many letters and sounds can the student do in a minute without help?

The dog runs. It catches a little rabbit. It brings the	11
little rabbit to Mom and Dad. Mom and Dad jump. No,	22
Dog! No rabbits! The dog goes. It sees a truck. Ruff!	33
Ruff! The dog wants to get the truck. No, Dog! Mom	44
and Dad are mad. Then a bad man comes. Ruff! Grrr!	55
The dog tackles the bad man. The bad man quits and	66
runs away. Good dog!	70

C. Listening

Ask each student individually without gestures of any kind. How many questions out of the total does the student respond correctly to?

1. Who are the people in your family?
2. Do you have any brothers and sisters?
3. What does your dad like to do?
4. What does your mom like to eat?
5. What do you like to do?
6. What do you like to eat?
7. Do you like French fries?
8. Do you like salad?
9. Are you tired?
10. Are you happy or sad today?

D. Spelling

See how many words the students can spell correctly. The teacher says the words one by one and the students spell the words out.

fat	see	day
cake	two	play
take	train	come

Unit 5

Speaking Practice
Practice until students can say the words individually without help.

What are you doing?
I am _____.

1.  looking for something	2.  helping someone	3.  going to get a pencil	4.  thinking
5.  eating a snack	6.  playing a game	7.  singing a song	8.  goofing off

Speaking Practice

Ask "What are you doing?" and point to a picture for the students to answer. Practice as a class and then check in with students individually.

Sign or Stamp

Reading Comprehension
Read, write, draw and color.

This is Fred. Fred plays with a red train. Fred has a plane too. The plane goes fast. Do you see the train and the plane?

1. Practice as a class. 2. Practice individually. 3. Sign or stamp only when the student can read it on their own without help.

e_e
ee
ea

these
here
tree
seed
read
clean

Spelling Words:
these
here
tree
read
clean

Sight Words:
all
there

Sign or Stamp

Students can work on this while you test them one on one on the previous page.

Write and find.

THESE   SEED   ALL

HERE   READ   THERE

TREE   CLEAN   PLAY

1. Practice as a class. 2. Practice individually. 3. Sign or stamp only when the student can read it on their own without help.

All these kids sit there in a tree. They sit and read. That is an odd spot to sit and read, kids.

Sign or Stamp

Students can work on this while you test them one on one on the previous page.

Unit 6

Speaking Practice

Practice until students can say the words individually without help.

What are you doing?
I am _____.

1. practicing my sentences

2. driving a car

3. climbing a tree

4. choosing a book

5. writing my worksheet

6. throwing a ball

7. making a paper airplane

8. flying

Listening Practice

Practice the questions together and then check in with students individually on their listening.

1. What are you doing?
2. Are you driving a car?
3. Are you practicing your sentences?
4. What do you like to eat?
5. How old are you?

Sign or Stamp

Reading Comprehension
Read, write, draw and color.

This is a big tree. His name is Tom. He is an apple tree. He has six red apples and three green apples on his branches.

1. Practice as a class. 2. Practice individually. 3. Sign or stamp only when the student can read it on their own without help.

i_e
ie
igh

hike
fine
die
tie
night
flight

Sight Words:
bear
says

Spelling Words:
five
time
die
night
says

Sign or Stamp

Students can work on this while you test them one on one on the previous page.

Write and find.

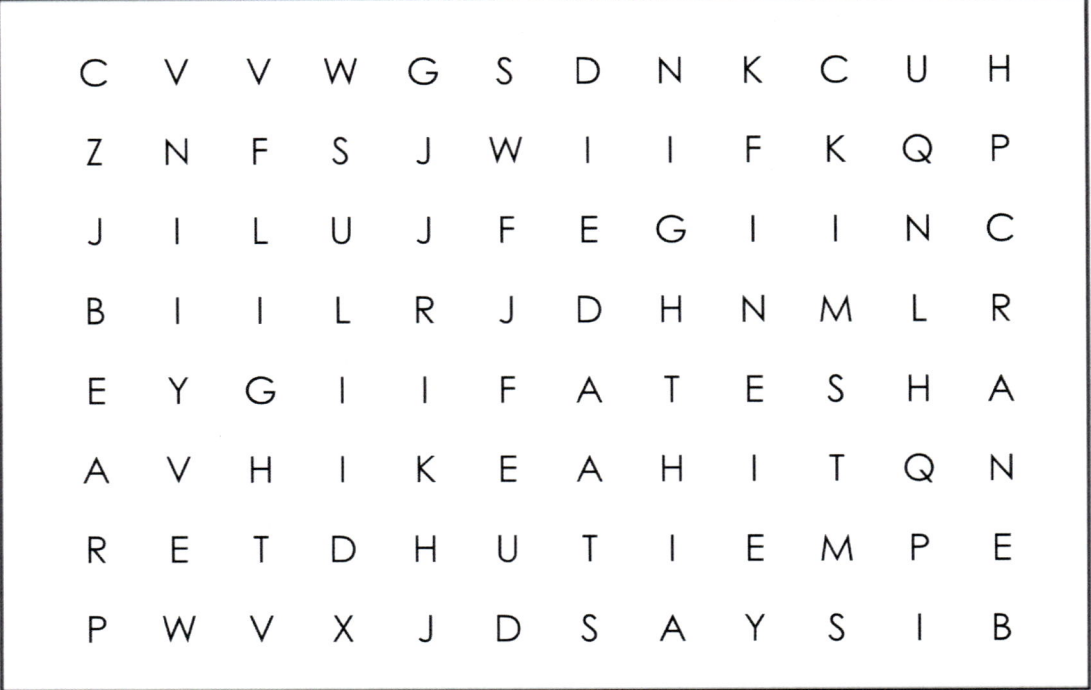

HIKE	TIE	BEAR
FINE	NIGHT	SAYS
DIE	FLIGHT	CRANE

1. Practice as a class. 2. Practice individually. 3. Sign or stamp only when the student can read it on their own without help.

The bear looks at the sign on the tree. The sign says, "You are here." The bear thinks that is not a big help.

Sign or Stamp

Students can work on this while you test them one on one on the previous page.

Unit 7

Speaking Practice

Practice until students can say the words individually without help.

What day is today?
It is _____.

1.
1
Monday

2.
2
Tuesday

3.
3
Wednesday

4.
4
Thursday

5.
5
Friday

6.
6
Saturday

7.
7
Sunday

8.
week

Listening Practice

Practice the questions together and then check in with students individually on their listening.

1. What are you doing?
2. Are you eating a snack?
3. What day is it today?
4. What does your dad like to do?
5. What is your favorite animal?

Sign or Stamp

Reading Comprehension

Read, write and color the monsters the correct color.

These are Kreegs. One green Kreeg is playing with a ball. One black Kreeg is sleeping. One pink Kreeg is digging.

1. Practice as a class. 2. Practice individually. 3. Sign or stamp only when the student can read it on their own without help.

_ _ _ _ y

_ _ y

happy

puppy

silly

my

fly

cry

Sight Words:

balloon

find

Spelling Words:
happy
silly
fly
cry

Sign or Stamp

Students can work on this while you test them one on one on the previous page.

Write and find.

HAPPY

MY

BALLOON

PUPPY

FLY

FIND

SILLY

CRY

NIGHT

1. Practice as a class. 2. Practice individually. 3. Sign or stamp only when the student can read it on their own without help.

My silly puppy likes to fly. He ties balloons to his body and goes up in the sky. Wait! I can't find my puppy and I want to cry.

Sign or Stamp

Students can work on this while you test them one on one on the previous page.

Unit 8

Speaking Practice

Practice until students can say the words individually without help.

When do you _____?
I _____ _____.

1.
brush your teeth

2.
take a shower

3.
go to bed

4.
eat dinner

5.
in the morning

6.
in the afternoon

7.
in the evening

8.
at night

Listening Practice

Practice the questions together and then check in with students individually on their listening.

1. When do you brush your teeth?
2. When do you go to bed?
3. When do you eat dinner?
4. When do you fight monsters?

Sign or Stamp

Reading Comprehension

Read, write and color the faces on the kids.

The kids play a game. Jen wins the game. She is happy. Ted did not win. He is sad. He needs to play the game more to get good.

1. Practice as a class. 2. Practice individually. 3. Sign or stamp only when the student can read it on their own without help.

o_e

oa

ow

bone

home

boat

float

blow

crow

Sight Words:

was

now

Spelling Words:
home
road
boat
blow

Sign or Stamp

Students can work on this while you test them one on one on the previous page.

Write and find.

BONE

FLOAT

WAS

HOME

BLOW

NOW

BOAT

CROW

HAPPY

1. Practice as a class. 2. Practice individually. 3. Sign or stamp only when the student can read it on their own without help.

His boat was floating and then it got a hole. Now the boat is sinking. The man hopes that he can swim to shore.

Sign or Stamp

Students can work on this while you test them one on one on the previous page.

Review Assessments

A. Speaking

1. Practice as a class and in partners beforehand.
2. How many sentences can you make in a minute?

1. (question)	3. (question)	5. (question)	7. (question)
2. (answer)	4. (answer)	6. (answer)	8. (answer)

9. (question)	11. (question)	13. (question)	15. (question)
10. (answer)	12. (answer)	14. (answer)	16. (answer)

17. (question)	19. (question)	21. (question)	23. (question)
18. (answer)	20. (answer)	22. (answer)	24. (answer)

Review Assessments

B. Reading

How many letters and sounds can the student do in a minute without help?

The mom makes a big cake. She puts the cake on a	12
tray in a box. She puts a string on the box. She takes	25
the cake to the train. She puts the cake on the train.	37
The train goes fast. A bad man plays with the cake.	48
He hits it. He smashes it. What a bad man! When the	60
train gets there, the cake is a mess. The mom is so	72
sad. What a day!	76

C. Listening

Ask each student individually without gestures of any kind. How many questions out of the total does the student respond correctly to?

1. What are you doing?
2. Are you driving a car?
3. When do you brush your teeth?
4. What do you like to eat?
5. How old are you?
6. Are you eating a snack?
7. What day is it today?
8. When do you eat dinner?
9. What does your dad like to do?
10. What is your favorite color?

D. Spelling

See how many words the students can spell correctly. The teacher says the words one by one and the students spell the words out.

these	five	home
tree	time	road
read	night	blow
clean	bear	boat

Unit 9

Speaking Practice

Practice until students can say the words individually without help.

How is the weather in _____?
It is _____.

1.
January

2.
February

3.
March

4.
April

5.
snowy

6.
cloudy

7.
windy

8.
rainy

Listening Practice

Practice the questions together and then check in with students individually on their listening.

1. How is the weather in January?
2. Is it hot in February?
3. How is the weather in April?
4. Do you like the weather in March?

Sign or Stamp

Reading Comprehension
Read, write and color the faces on the kids.

This is a very funny thing. The man is staying in the dog's home, and the dog is staying in the man's home. That is so silly!

1. Practice as a class. 2. Practice individually. 3. Sign or stamp only when the student can read it on their own without help.

u_e
ue
ui

tube
flute
blue
true
suit
fruit

Sight Words:
her
does

Sometimes:
cute
cube

Spelling Words:
cute
blue
fruit
does

Sign or Stamp

Students can work on this while you test them one on one on the previous page.

Write and find.

TUBE TRUE HER

FLUTE SUIT DOES

BLUE FRUIT HOME

1. Practice as a class. 2. Practice individually. 3. Sign or stamp only when the student can read it on their own without help.

The kid has a suit and plays the flute with her lips. The moose does not have a suit and plays the flute with its nose.

Sign or Stamp

Students can work on this while you test them one on one on the previous page.

Unit 10

Speaking Practice

Practice until students can say the words individually without help.

What do you do in _____?
I _____.

1.

5
May

2.

6
June

3.

7
July

4.

8
August

5.
go on vacation

6.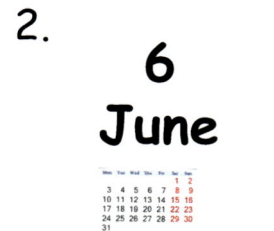
go camping

7.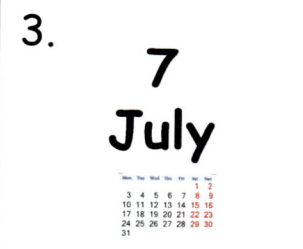
go to the beach

8.
stay home

Listening Practice

Practice the questions together and then check in with students individually on their listening.

1. What do you do in July?
2. How is the weather in August?
3. What do you do in May?
4. How is the weather in June?

Sign or Stamp

Reading Comprehension
Read, write and color the faces on the kids.

It is May. It is rainy. A kid is in the rain. She has an umbrella. She is running home. She wants to get inside quick.

1. Practice as a class. 2. Practice individually. 3. Sign or stamp only when the student can read it on their own without help.

oo
ew

boot
troop
hoop
new
flew
chew

Sight Words:
know
some

Sometimes:
book
look

Spelling Words:
look
took
new
flew

Sign or Stamp

Students can work on this while you test them one on one on the previous page.

Write and find.

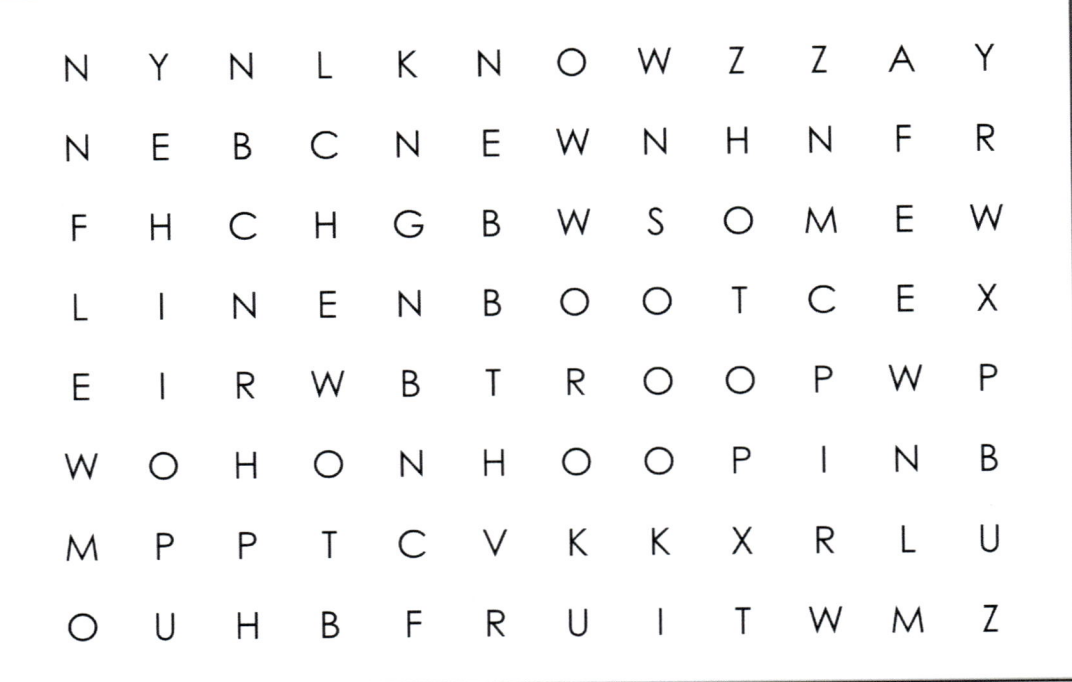

BOOT

NEW

KNOW

TROOP

FLEW

SOME

HOOP

CHEW

FRUIT

1. Practice as a class. 2. Practice individually. 3. Sign or stamp only when the student can read it on their own without help.

That does not look like a strong knight. He needs a new suit and some new boots too. I know that dragon will eat him, and I think that donkey knows it too.

Sign or Stamp

Students can work on this while you test them one on one on the previous page.

Unit 11

Speaking Practice

Practice until students can say the words individually without help.

What do you do in _____?
I _____.

1. September 	2. October 	3. November 	4. December 
5.  go to school	6.  have piano lessons	7.  take tests	8.  celebrate Christmas

Listening Practice

Practice the questions together and then check in with students individually on their listening.

1. What do you do in September?
2. How is the weather in October?
3. What do you do in December?
4. Do you take tests in November?
5. What are the months of the year?

Sign or Stamp

Reading Comprehension
Read, write and color the faces on the kids.

Sally likes to read. She has many books. Here are two of her books. One book is on fish. The other book is on boats.

1. Practice as a class. 2. Practice individually. 3. Sign or stamp only when the student can read it on their own without help.

ou
ow

house
trout
mouth
now
down
clown

Sight Words:
through
tiger

Careful!

blow
slow

Spelling Words:
house
mouth
how
down

Sign or Stamp

Students can work on this while you test them one on one on the previous page.

Write and find.

HOUSE	NOW	THROUGH
TROUT	DOWN	TIGER
MOUTH	CLOWN	BOOK

1. Practice as a class. 2. Practice individually. 3. Sign or stamp only when the student can read it on their own without help.

The cute clown shouts for the tiger to jump through the hoop. The tiger thinks, "How am I going to do that? If you like this hoop so much, you jump through it!"

Sign or Stamp

Students can work on this while you test them one on one on the previous page.

Unit 12

Speaking Practice

Practice until students can say the words individually without help.

What time do you _____?
I _____ at _____.

1.  get up
2.  eat breakfast
3.  eat lunch
4.  get out of school
5.
6.
7.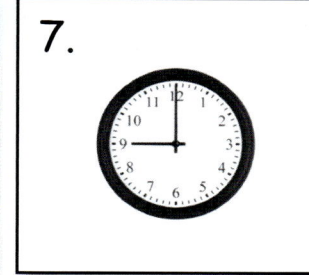
8.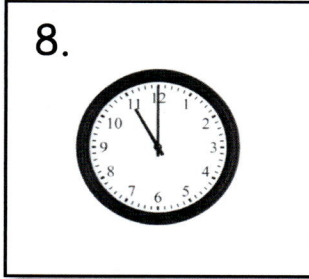

Listening Practice

Practice the questions together and then check in with students individually on their listening.

1. What time do you get up in the morning?
2. What time do you eat breakfast?
3. What time do you eat lunch?
4. What time do you get out of school?
5. What time is class over?

Sign or Stamp

Reading Comprehension
Read, write and color the faces on the kids.

Betty the cow can fly. She is Super Cow. Betty the SuperCow is blue. She will catch the bad dog. The bad dog is taking food!

1. Practice as a class. 2. Practice individually. 3. Sign or stamp only when the student can read it on their own without help.

er
ir
ur

her
faster
bird
birthday
surf
purple

Sight Words:
water
goes

Spelling Words:
her
bird
purple
goes

Sign or Stamp

Students can work on this while you test them one on one on the previous page.

Write and find.

HER

BIRTHDAY

WATER

FASTER

SURF

GOES

BIRD

PURPLE

COUCH

1. Practice as a class. 2. Practice individually. 3. Sign or stamp only when the student can read it on their own without help.

This bird gets its board. It gets its swim trunks. It goes out on the water. Look at that bird go! It is faster than a boat. Wow! This bird can surf!

Sign or Stamp

Students can work on this while you test them one on one on the previous page.

Review Assessments

A. Speaking

1. Practice as a class and in partners beforehand.
2. How many sentences can you make in a minute?

1. (question) 2. (answer)	3. (question) 4. (answer)	5. (question) 6. (answer)	7. (question) 8. (answer)

1 January **2** February **3** March **4** April

9. (question) 10. (answer)	11. (question) 12. (answer)	13. (question) 14. (answer)	15. (question) 16. (answer)

5 May  **6** June  **7** July  **8** August

17. (question) 18. (answer)	19. (question) 20. (answer)	21. (question) 22. (answer)	23. (question) 24. (answer)

Review Assessments

B. Reading

How many letters and sounds can the student do in a minute without help?

There are nine cats in the night. They run and play	11
and screech. The nine cats often fight. They fight as	21
they see things to eat. One cat with the name Tom	32
thinks, "This is not right. This stinks. Let us share the	43
things to eat, please, and let us share the things to	54
drink." The cats say, "OK! Good job, Tom!" and those	64
cats are as happy as can be.	71

C. Listening

Ask each student individually without gestures of any kind. How many questions out of the total does the student respond correctly to?

1. How is the weather in January?
2. Is it hot in February?
3. What do you do in September?
4. What time do you get up in the morning?
5. What do you do in July?
6. How is the weather in August?
7. What time do you get out of school?
8. What time do you go to bed?

D. Spelling

See how many words the students can spell correctly. The teacher says the words one by one and the students spell the words out.

blue	new	how
fruit	flew	her
look	house	bird
took	mouth	purple

Unit 13

Speaking Practice

Practice until students can say the words individually without help.

Why is the _____ happy?
Because the _____ is _____.

1.  pirate	2.  witch	3.  ghost	4.  princess
5.  sailing a ship	6.  riding a broom	7.  scaring people	8.  kissing a prince

Listening Practice

Practice the questions together and then check in with students individually on their listening.

1. Why is the witch happy?
2. Why is the ghost happy?
3. Why are you happy?
4. What time do you go to bed?
5. What do you do in July?

Sign or Stamp

Reading Comprehension
Read, write and color the faces on the kids.

There are three birds in the tree. One is blue, one is green and one is red. A cat wants to eat the birds. Where is the cat?

1. Practice as a class. 2. Practice individually. 3. Sign or stamp only when the student can read it on their own without help.

ar
all

car
star
hard
all
ball
stall

Sight Words:
because
other

Spelling Words:
star
hard
ball

Sign or Stamp

Students can work on this while you test them one on one on the previous page.

Write and find.

CAR   ALL   BECAUSE

STAR   BALL   OTHER

HARD   STALL   PURPLE

1. Practice as a class. 2. Practice individually. 3. Sign or stamp only when the student can read it on their own without help.

This girl drives a blue car with a star on it, and she goes fast. She goes faster than all the other cars. Vroom! She wins and she smiles because she is just that good.

Sign or Stamp

Students can work on this while you test them one on one on the previous page.

Unit 14

Speaking Practice

Practice until students can say the words individually without help.

Where is she going?
She is going to the _____.

1. police station

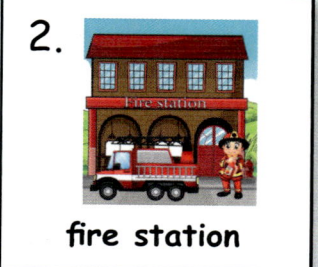
2. fire station

3. pet shop

4. grocery store

5. park

6. swimming pool

7. mall

8. movie theater

Listening Practice

Practice the questions together and then check in with students individually on their listening.

1. Where is your mom going?
2. Where are you going?
3. Where do you want to go?
4. Why is the pirate happy?
5. What do you do in December?

Sign or Stamp

Reading Comprehension
Read, write and color the faces on the kids.

This is Bill the clown. He is driving a purple car. He has blue hair. He has a red nose. Bill is so funny!

1. Practice as a class. 2. Practice individually. 3. Sign or stamp only when the student can read it on their own without help.

au
aw

cause
August
haunt
saw
fawn
draw

Sight Words:
ghost
away

Spelling Words:
because
saw
draw
away

Students can work on this while you test them one on one on the previous page.

Write and find.

CAUSE

SAW

GHOST

AUGUST

FAWN

AWAY

HAUNT

DRAW

CALL

1. Practice as a class. 2. Practice individually. 3. Sign or stamp only when the student can read it on their own without help.

"Ghosts haunt this house," Beth says. "How do you know?" asks Jack. "Because I saw them!" Beth says. "Ghosts are not real!" says Jack. "Boo!" says Beth. "Ahhhh!" Jack says as he runs away.

Sign or Stamp

Students can work on this while you test them one on one on the previous page.

Unit 15

Speaking Practice

Practice until students can say the words individually without help.

What's wrong?

_____.

1.  I have a cold.	2. 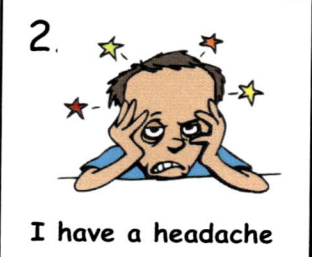 I have a headache.	3.  I have a stomachache.	4.  I have the runs.
5.  I have a mosquito bite.	6. 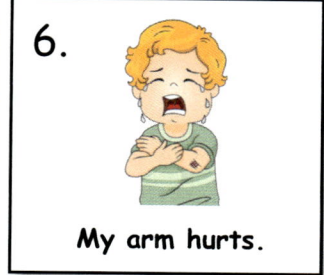 My arm hurts.	7.  My leg hurts.	8. 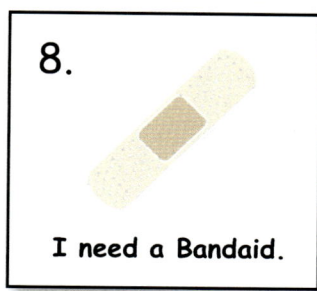 I need a Bandaid.

Listening Practice

Practice the questions together and then check in with students individually on their listening.

1. What's wrong?
2. Why is the princess happy?
3. What do you wear in January?
4. What time do you go to school?

Sign or Stamp

Reading Comprehension
Read, write and color the faces on the kids.

This is a farm. There is a cow. There is a rabbit. There is a pig. There is a farmer. Can you draw them all?

1. Practice as a class. 2. Practice individually. 3. Sign or stamp only when the student can read it on their own without help.

oi
oy

oil
point
noisy
boy
enjoy
oyster

Sight Words:
people
annoy

Spelling Words:
noisy
boy
enjoy
people

Sign or Stamp

Students can work on this while you test them one on one on the previous page.

Write and find.

OIL

BOY

PEOPLE

POINT

ENJOY

ANNOY

NOISY

OYSTER

SAW

1. Practice as a class. 2. Practice individually. 3. Sign or stamp only when the student can read it on their own without help.

This noisy boy's name is John. John enjoys annoying his brother Sam. John is so loud that Sam's ears hurt. "Stop being so noisy, John!" says Sam. "It's not funny! I think people down the street can hear you!"

Sign or Stamp

Students can work on this while you test them one on one on the previous page.

Review Assessments

A. Speaking

1. Practice as a class and in partners beforehand.
2. How many sentences can you make in a minute?

1. (question)   3. (question)   5. (question)   7. (question)
2. (answer)   4. (answer)   6. (answer)   8. (answer)

9. (question)   11. (question)   13. (question)   15. (question)
10. (answer)   12. (answer)   14. (answer)   16. (answer)

17. (question)   19. (question)   21. (question)   23. (question)
18. (answer)   20. (answer)   22. (answer)   24. (answer)

  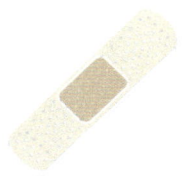 

Review Assessments

B. Reading

How many letters and sounds can the student do in a minute without help?

> A boy saw a star. "I want to fly to that star," said the boy. "It can't be too hard." The boy found a car. He drove the car. "Nope, that will not work." Next, he found a boat. He got in the boat. "Nope, that will not work." He saw a plane. He flew the plane. "That star is hard to reach," he said. He went to bed. He had a dream. He went to the star. He was happy.

14
26
36
48
59
72
81

C. Listening

Ask each student individually without gestures of any kind. How many questions out of the total does the student respond correctly to?

1. Where is your mom going?
2. Where are you going?
3. Where do you want to go?
4. Why is the witch happy?
5. What do you do in December?
6. What time do you go to bed?
7. What do you do in July?
8. What's wrong?

D. Spelling

See how many words the students can spell correctly. The teacher says the words one by one and the students spell the words out.

star	saw	people
hard	noisy	because
ball	boy	away
draw	enjoy	

Copyright 2021

Kid-Inspired Classroom

All rights reserved. No part of this book may be reproduced in any form.

Made in the USA
Monee, IL
04 May 2024

57904842R00059